The Wildly Quiet
Presence Of God

Additional Books by Ragini Elizabeth Michaels

*Unflappable – 6 Steps To Staying Happy, Centered,
& Peaceful No Matter What* (2012)
Conari Press, San Francisco, CA

Lions In Wait – a road to personal courage (1993)
Facticity Trainings, Inc. Seattle, WA

Facticity – a door to mental health & beyond (1991)
Facticity Trainings, Inc., Seattle, WA

The Wildly Quiet Presence Of God

— MUSINGS OF A MODERN MARKETPLACE MYSTIC —

Ragini Elizabeth Michaels

ISBN: 1511457651
ISBN 13: 9781511457651

Library of Congress Control Number: 2015905350

Create Space Independent Publishing Platform
North Charleston, South Carolina

Dedication

To that amazing inner magnetic pull that guides
us toward Home so we can finally set up permanent residence
deep in the middle of Here and Now

"Love tells me I am everything.
Wisdom tells me I am nothing.
Between these two, my life flows."

Sri Nisargadatta

Table of Contents

Foreword

This collection of verses carries the scent of a mystic. It seems that all is said here, with sparks of wisdom and an open heart, as well as the vulnerability and the magnificence of being human. Ragini is a true spiritual seeker and mystic of our times. Mystics are hard to find, and perhaps a woman mystic even rarer.

But in this time and age, we need the tenderness combined with sharpness of mind, which Ragini generously pours into this little book. I would rather just sing my praises for Ragini. But I know she would be shy and would say 'stop' once again, and with a grin or a smile touch my soul.

I hope your soul, dear reader, is touched as you read these musings. They are simple and sincere. They are also deep and profound. With Ragini, one cannot get away from her love of dancing with polarities. So, with this depth of understanding throughout these verses, Ragini shares her blessing as a shining chandelier of sparkling light to whomever is around. You are a lucky reader to meet up with this modern day mystic.

It is a great honor and a humbling experience to write this foreword because Ragini has been a teacher to me, as well as a friend. I owe her through her work in NLP, and as a leading expert on the subject, the deepening of my understanding in a practical way of Madhyamika (a cornerstone of Mahayana Buddhist philosophy) as well as the main idea for my PhD thesis.

Christian Palocz, PhD
Paris, France 3 May 2015
El Tibet y el mundo entero: El Conflicto Tibetano-Chino Desde Una Perspectivea No Dual
2011, Cuarto Propio, Santiago, Chile
Tibet And The World: The Tibetan-Chinese Conflict From A Non-Dual Perspective

Dear Friend,

I selected these 40 offerings from over 100 poems and musings written over the course of 10 years. As I traveled the path of my personal, professional, and spiritual journeys, I cried, laughed, and suffered. I endured the throes of depression, longed for more exquisite tastes of a promised bliss, and searched for the serenity a conscious life says it offers. It's been quite an expedition, full of learning and discovering.

Each year I gathered up my thoughts and paired them with images to create a calendar for my students and friends. I've now placed 40 of these pairings into this volume – the first of three (hopefully) sharing all 120 ponderings. I hope they are able to offer you some support, laughter, and inspiration for your own exploration of conscious living in daily life.

If you fall into the belief you're not doing your journey right, doing it too slow, or are just not capable of ever reaching the cherished goal of Truth, Love, and Freedom, these musings are for you.

I can only say my best course of action has been to keep on following that inner pull. Today, I can honestly say it has led me to finally become friendly with that wildly quiet presence of God – and to know It is indeed real and not just a lovely idea.

Once I stopped feeling embarrassed about engaging in a love affair with the Divine, daily life became a whole lot easier. It is my hope that whatever your path in life, or towards the Divine, these musings will give you a laugh, a smile, or just a tiny touch of what we all seek – the knowing that we are also a wildly quiet presence of God.

In love and gratitude,
Ragini

Acknowledgements

Thanks to my family, friends, and students who have supported me and loved me even when they didn't understand what I was doing or why.

While I took many of the photos, I want to thank contributors Andy Olney and the folks who offer their lovely photos, free of charge and without attribution at www.MorgueFile.com. Without your talent and generosity, this book would not carry such visual beauty.

Thanks to Suryo Gardner and Sondra Kornblatt for their time and energy proofing these verses and for their encouragement to share them in this form.

And finally, deep gratitude to my friend, Sudipo Lee Congdon, who shared her discovery of what has become my next step in this amazing journey.

Much gratitude and love to each of you.
Ragini

Confessions

When I Am Still

When I am still
and hear the snow falling
And notice moon's shadows glistening on white

I feel the company
Of a silent Presence
Holding my hand.

Then ... I'm so glad
I listened to my
Ridiculous desire to
Believe in the unbelievable.

I Do Realize

I do realize no thought, no idea, no concept at all,
can hold a candle to the brilliant genius
of nature and its striking attention to detail.

Still, my mind does struggle to compete—
creating the most dazzling and dramatic stories
of personal agony and ecstasy.

But if it's ok, I think I'd rather just sit still now—
and be stunned into graceful silence
by the gifted virtuosity of Life.

When The Formless Decided

When the formless
decided
to take on form,
I wish
it would have
included labels
that said
"Made Of God"
with a tag
that said
"Do Not Remove
Under Penalty

of Law".

Then
maybe
we wouldn't be
so careless
with our bodies
or
with
each other.

I Keep Catching Glimpses

I keep catching glimpses of what those mystics
are always talking about.

But the fact is, I'm too afraid to come out of hiding
and grab them from behind and make them stay around
for a while.

I guess I'll just have to wait until my lion's heart
decides to roar and scares them into setting up camp
in my neck of the woods.

I Didn't Know You Were Going To Join Me

I didn't know You were going to
join me at my table.

I don't think Your game
of hide and seek
is working well any more.

You seem to have
lost Your knack
for staying out of sight.

You see, I keep spotting You
slipping in and out of view.

I know how much You

enjoy this silly game of
"Come and Find Me
If You Can!"

But I need a bit more courage
to face the thought of
seeing You
without a hitch.

I can't imagine what a madwoman I'm going to be
when I can see You everywhere.

Honestly, I didn't know You were going to join me at my table
or I most certainly would have prepared
a place for You.

All Things Are Just Waiting To Be Used

All things are just waiting to be used—for someone to need
what they have been designed to do—

How can a chair find satisfaction if no one ever surrenders to rest
and discovers the cozy comfort of its emptiness?

How can a cup display its function
without someone first encountering their thirst?

All things want to be used. And that includes me . . .
And . . . I would guess . . . you too.

I'm quietly waiting now, to be used again

For some reason, I grew tired.

I think I needed time

to empty out
and fill up again
with space.

Now I'm waiting—

praying actually
to be used yet again.

To enjoy
my purpose for being,

I guess
I'll have to hang out my
"Open for Business" sign
one more time.

I'm Trying To Remember

I'm trying
to remember.
The dragons

of this day
are not as large
or as powerful
as I think

After all,
My Beloved keeps
telling me
I *am*
The Dragon Slayer,

The One
Who Slays

With Love
And
Presence.

But I don't think
I can do these amazing feats without
My Dearest One.

Perhaps,
if I'm still,
You will be
kind enough
to appear
by my side.

No Matter The Number

No matter the number of shadows
dancing round the universe,
there can't ever be enough
to snuff out the light
of a single candle.

Still, I keep forgetting.
The same is true for this Light
glowing in my own heart and soul

No matter how long
darkness licks its chops
on the circumference
of its radiance,

this Light remains
unconcerned
and holds steady—
whether I'm aware of it
or not.

Doesn't that mean
I'm
being
taken
care of,
despite
what
I
might
think?

Every Day At Least Once Or Twice

Every day, at least once or twice, I get caught up in the idea
that I'm totally in charge of my life!

A compulsion grips me and I'm forced to try and
make something happen—fast!

The idea I have this kind of responsibility sort of
puts a damper on my sense of freedom.

I'm so glad Wisdom grabs my ear and tells me to make my efforts—
take action—and then— relax and let things be as they are.

It's kind of wonderful
when I remember I don't have to constantly *do*.

I never would have thought
taking time
to just *be*
could be included
in my cosmic job description.

What a blessed relief
to know my relaxing isn't the same as
Atlas shrugging
and dropping
the whole world
on its
head.

It's Captivating

It's captivating how the bench simply sits—
beautifully empty—patiently waiting.

I wonder … does it long for the time
when it will be of use
once again?

I've been advised
(over and over I'm afraid) to please
stop asking such questions and just emulate the bench.

But I have to tell you.

I don't find it as easy as that bench makes it look

Courting Contradictions

I Really Love How Darkness

I really love how Darkness flexes its creative muscles in the winter.
I fancy the artistic bent it displays in the simple complexity
of an icy chill, or the shadow designs
stretched frozen in snow.

I think Nature is grand
to give the oft maligned
Darkness its due
in such
a gorgeous way—
even though
it *is* a bit on
the cold side.

I must confess
there are days
I get a bit cranky about this frosty state of affairs
and earnestly wish Darkness were *not*
the keeper of the Light.

But then wisdom jogs my memory
and I'm reminded Darkness and Light
are really hot and heavy into this on-going love affair.

And I guess we all know
it's never a good idea to get caught up in someone else's love affair
by taking sides.

I think I'll just pull out another blanket and cozy up to the fire.

It's funny how knowing winter is really all about Love
makes me feel warm on the inside.

Please Come Close To Me

When I hear myself say, "Please come close
to me—BUT—Keep your distance!"

I know I have to
balance
these two desires—
for only then can
Divine Love
be free
to come out of hiding.

In The Summer I Love To Seek

In the summer,
I love to seek out
the shade's reprieve
so I can get
soaked to the skin
in its coolness!

In the winter,
I'm drawn the other way.

As that perfect
shaft of daylight
creeps across the floor,
I love to stretch out and
marinate my body in
its warmth.

But it's truly grand when my focus grabs hold
of both the light and the dark as a seamless whole!

I'm enthralled by their wild spontaneous frolic against my walls
when the wind blows through the trees—
and their precision teamwork when the sun
spills through the blinds.

They fashion such stellar black and white
medleys of stillness and motion that even the boldest color
is forced to step to the side for a while.

My heart and mind are really into learning this seamless two-step.

They're still a bit clumsy—
but we're definitely
having fun!

It's Too Bad

It's too bad
Getting centered
And feeling balanced
Can't last forever.

Seems all that
Wobbling is necessary
To keep us steady.

It Hasn't Escaped My Notice

It hasn't escaped my notice that the Sun and the Moon don't argue—
and the Ocean and the Shore don't fight. So I guess I'm
a little embarrassed that I'm pissed off at You.

But my greed has gotten the better of me today because I'm plum out
of gratitude! I just want to live in this Light of Yours *all* the time!

You keep arriving and then departing and it makes me mad!
I'm tired of making up my guest room over and over.
Can't You just move in permanently?

Oh well. My temper tantrums never change a thing. Everything comes
and then it goes—including my ability to stay connected to You!

But just so You know, I'm following that advice You gave me and
actually enjoying my little display of temper. Being such a
feisty individual *is* kind of fun!

Acceptance Keeps Dressing Up As Love

Acceptance keeps dressing up as Love . . .
And getting away with it—

Until Rejection comes along
And rips off its disguise.

It's best to let them play this game of hide n' seek without me
And focus instead
On finding the real doorway Home.

Being In The Spotlight

Being in the spotlight
can be completely
discombobulating!

Part of me hides
& another revels in that glorious shower of attention.

But here's the thing—
When I find that
sweet spot
where the two
share a common truth,
I see them
happily dancing
together— conflict gone!

Maybe there is something
to this
'Middle Way' thing
after all.

We Inhabit Two Worlds

We inhabit
two worlds—
inner and outer.

Like our breath—both in and out
are required.

I've discovered it's best to embrace each
as you would
a lover
giving you
the grandest
orgasm
of your life!

Wayward Rocks Strewn Haphazardly

It's strange . . . wayward rocks strewn haphazardly
don't meet my criteria for chaos.

But my errant thoughts, dedicated to
bedlam and aimless wandering,
definitely claim the prize.

Yet, when I catch a glimpse of disorder's beauty & valor,
chaos quietly slips into its rightful place
as order's most genteel and coveted companion.

All My Fellow Mystics

All my fellow mystics say Duality isn't the final word on the real nature of Reality. They keep saying Duality is an illusion. I have to agree it *is* the best darn sleight of hand I've ever encountered!

But as far as my mind and body are concerned,
Duality is *definitely* the real deal.

I hope my heart succeeds in its quest to bring my mind and body on board. Not understanding reality and illusion are friendly playmates can be awfully painful.

Perhaps when my heart succeeds, I'll be able to enjoy this enchanting merry-go-round ride with a bit more relish and delight

Gestures Of The Divine

The Amazing Precision

The amazing precision of
Nature's patterns
makes me breathe a sigh of relief.

Something akin to what I call
Intelligence
must be in operation—
That helps me grasp the notion that I am
an equally elegant motif—
obviously
created
by
Divine
design.

When Joy Appears To Be Eluding Me

When Joy appears to be eluding me,
I rush to search under the couch cushions
and under my chair.

I even go through my kitchen cupboards and my old photo albums—
but more often than not, it remains nowhere to be found.

I realize I must have inadvertently closed up shop
due to some inclement weather in my heart.

Then I just have to make do with Faith—and trust
that sunny skies
will appear in the forecast
sometime
again
soon.

I Think It Takes Courage

I think it takes courage
to venture into the dark.

So I make certain
I always take a bit of light with me.

I am grateful
for each small flicker
of illumination.

When I can see through my fear,
I am awed
by what
the shadows
are willing to
tell me.

Like The Rest Of Nature

Like the rest
Of Nature,
I am
Beginning to
Move inward
In preparation
For the winter—

At the
Same time
I know this
Inward movement
Is an outward
Stretch as well—
Reaching
Through

The cold months
To my new beginnings
Just ahead.

How good
It feels
To know
I am
In the hands
Of this
Grand
Scheme
Called
Life.

These Days Clarity Emerges

These days
Clarity emerges in my perception
As a gentle unfolding—

Like the delicate gesture
Of a deferential geisha,
The hand of the universe
Gracefully spreads across my awareness
A beautiful and complexly organized understanding that—
Like a flash of lightening—is here and gone.

It is such an exquisite form of communication
That I have no doubt it is really
Communion
In
Disguise.

There Is A Precise Instant When Ripeness Arises

There is a precise
instant when
ripeness arises—
When all the
essentials
merge into a
seamless partnering
of perfection.

But what stuns me most
is how this moment of rightness
keeps coming to pass
Again and Again

There Is Something So Sweet

There is something
so sweet
about this bicycle—
just leaning there
against the fence.

Sometimes I just want to lean against
something too.
If I can't find God,
then a person,
or even a tree, will do.
It doesn't seem
to matter
as long as
the sweetness is there—
and the remembrance
I'm not here all alone.

It Seems The Rain Drops Congregrate

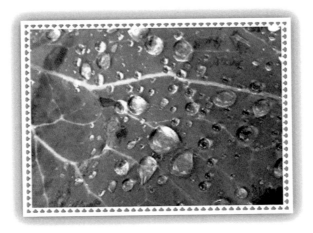

It seems the rain drops congregate
to display their diverse talents for reflection.

Not to be outdone,
I decide to reflect anew on some of my
worn-out story lines.

They've been pestering me
for a while now
with their urgent need
for a wiser and
more illuminating way
of seeing things.

Letting Go Of Anything

Letting go of anything
is a frightening proposition for my mind.

Still—the grace and beauty
emanating from the curve
of a bowed head
makes my heart and soul yearn
for their own taste of this sweet surrender.

Then I must endure
my mind's struggle with this longing
until the exhaustion bows my head for me.

It Is Beauty's Brush Strokes

It is
Beauty's
brush strokes
that make
God
and
Love
real enough
for me
to grasp my
doubt's hand—
and
together—
leap into faith.

Slivers Of Truth

I Love Those Days
I Wake Up Full

I love those days I wake up full of strength. I flex my emotional
muscles and feel nothing in the day can disturb
my sense of place in the world.

I'm not so fond of those mornings when I'm trembling with
fragility. Then I feel weak, and pretty shy about claiming
any space in this world.

Those are the days I've learned to imagine I'm a grand lioness,
endowed with a divine potency intrinsic to my form,
and a wisdom that perceives trembling
as nothing but the need to rest and re-energize.

So I rest.
And when I'm ready,

I glance up at the heavens to access my courage,

And then
I'm on the prowl—

trusting
I will meet the
lively challenges
I am born to chase down and
make
into
tasty food
for
my
soul.

The Beauty Of Nature's Patterns

The
Beauty of
Nature's Patterns
Brings me
A Sense of
Peace and
Restfulness

My mind
Quiets,
And I find
I've
Come home
To
Myself.

Last Night I Was So Drenched In Longing

Last night I was so drenched in longing
that I had to
climb out of bed
and go in search
of the moon.

When I found her
my heart got giddy
with joy.
I wanted to
leap out the window
and bank her brilliance,
like savings
for my retirement.

I felt alive with confidence and trust that I would always
get what I need.

But then the wind and the clouds arrived—
and her radiance and my faith vanished from view. My heart took a nose-
dive, and my joy sadly melted into sorrow.

I think this kind of emotional choreography is a bit difficult
to perform gracefully.

But I keep practicing
because my heart has visited that place,
miles beyond emotion,
where duality's dazzling dance becomes transparent.

You can't hide from me there, Dear One.
I see You,
smiling out at me
from behind Your clever disguise
as the Two.

I Awoke This Morning And Remembered

I awoke this morning
And remembered that
Gratefulness
Is the only balance
To my greedy
Insatiable
Gusto
For
Life.

I Love Snow's Silence Plummeting Down

I love snow's silence plummeting downward—
her crystal beauties
quieting the sounds of life—

lacy layers of grey and white
snuggling close to the earth's warmth.

As I witness this seduction of
Divine Stillness,

I hear serenity
shyly
stepping
forward.

Make Impermanence
Your Friend

Make
impermanence
your
friend.

Have an
intimate chat
over lunch.

When you realize
you can go
nowhere
without It,

You will
ride the waves
of
your
emotional
turmoil
with
Great
Artistry
and
Joy.

Embrace Your Discontent

Embrace your
everyday discontent.

Relax . . .

Munch on a carrot . . .

Inquire with a polite
question or two . . .

Pay the price of
Elegant Attention.

And then . . . savor the gift of
your discontent's wisdom.

You've been passing right by it for ever so long.

Life's Theatrics Are Quite Enlivening

Life's theatrics are quite Enlivening!
No way to discover if the day will bring
deep dramatic tension, or sweet comedic relief.

No way to know whether I'll be touched by a laugh or a tear.

Either way, it's best to write optimistic stories from now on—
even though I'm certain a few pessimistic ones
will wrangle their way in.

Life is so good at making *all* my stories
feel so incredibly real
that I'm quite likely to forget
none
are comments
on the nature of my soul.

Hope I'm up to the challenge of playing out my role
in this cosmic production.

.

It seems life can be a bit over-the-top when she feels free
to display the full range of her theatrical talents.

I just wish she weren't so committed to full self-expression
on such a consistent daily basis.

Faith Is The Rumble
Of Trust & Doubt

Faith
Is the
Rumble
Of
Trust and doubt—

Together,
They create the
Tension and relief
That marks
Faith
A Great Work of Art.

Beyond The Corridors Of Mind

Beyond the corridors of mind
Love of another dimension
Sets up housekeeping.

One visit here
Reveals why all shades of Beauty
Are really thieves
Out to steal your heart
And
Return
It
Home.

Photo Credit

To see more photos from each MorgueFile.com artist, write in the artist's name after the last forward slash in the following url and then go to http://www.morguefile.com/creative/

Confessions

When I Am Still - johnlindsay
I Do Realize - Ragini
When The Formless Decided - Jacky
I Keep Catching Glimpses - lucasmalta
I Didn't Know You Were Going To Join Me – unknown
All Things Are Just Waiting To Be Used - jade
I'm Trying To Remember - pinhed
No Matter The Number - rubencolorado
Every Day At Least Once Or Twice - rikahi
It's Captivating - Ragini

Courting Contradictions

I Really Love How Darkness - MarcoMaru
Please Come Close To Me - iStockPhoto
In The Summer I Love To Seek - Ragini
It's Too Bad - iStockPhoto
It Hasn't Escaped My Notice - hotblack

Acceptance Keeps Dressing Up As Love - iStockPhoto
Being In The Spotlight - Ragini
We Inhabit Two Worlds - iStockPhoto
Wayward Rocks Strewn Haphazardly - Ragini
All My Fellow Mystics - cinda

Gestures Of The Divine

The Amazing Precision - Brazilian
When Joy Appears To Be Eluding Me - AcrylicArtist
I Think It Takes Courage - rosevita
Like The Rest Of Nature - Ragini
These Days Clarity Emerges - pschubert
There Is A Precise Instant - Ragini
There Is Something So Sweet - Ragini
It Seems The Rain Drops Congregate - Ragini
Letting Go Of Anything - Ragini
It Is Beauty's Brush Strokes - Ragini

Slivers Of Truth

I Love Those Days I Wake Up Full - matthew_hull
The Beauty of Nature's Patterns - AcrylicArtist
Last Night I Was So Drenched In Longing - cooee
I Awoke This Morning and Remembered - veggiegretz
I Love Snow's Silence Plummeting Down - Ragini
Make Impermanence Your Friend - Ragini
Embrace Your Discontent -Andy Olney
Life's Theatrics - darkwombat
Faith Is The Rumble of Trust & Doubt - Ragini
Beyond The Corridors Of Mind - AcrylicArtist

About The Author

Ragini, most loved and appreciated for her work in *Paradox Management,* is also an internationally acclaimed trainer of Neuro-Linguistic Programming (NLP), and accomplished Hypnotherapist with a background in Physiological Psychology.

Her original work on the *Psychology of the Mystics* has received critical acclaim, taken her throughout America, Canada, Europe, and India presenting workshops and seminars, and evolved into her on-line training, *The Mystic's Wisdom: De-Coded.*

She is the creator of eight hypnosis/meditation MP3's in two series - *Hypnosis To Heal The Heart & Soul* and *Hypnosis For Conscious Awakening,* author of three earlier books on paradox and mystic psychology, and founder of the *Paradox Wisdom School,* Seattle, Washington, 2000-2010, using the Enneagram to better surf our dual identity as both human and divine.

Her approach to spirituality stems from her diverse professional background, and over forty years personally exploring meditation and contemplation, Vipassana retreats, trips to India, and years as a disciple of the eastern mystic, Osho.

Upon finally owning her mystical bent, she began to share her experiences of exploring spirituality and the power of viewing mundane life problems with an eye for mystical guidance and insight.

You can visit her at www.RaginiMichaels.com. For more information and trainings, please email rm@RaginiMichaels.com or call 001 425 462 4369.

Free Resources

Videos:

- *The Psychology of the Mystics* (the foundation of Unflappable)
  www.RaginiMichaels.com

- *Unflappable* (Book Trailer)
  www.Amazon.com/ragini-elizabeth-michaels

Audio:

- *Moving From Fear To Love* (free audio series)
  www.MovingFrom FearToLove.com

Please enjoy. And may you be happy, centered, and peaceful – no matter what.

Much love,
Ragini

Made in the USA
San Bernardino, CA
16 July 2015